# INDIAN WOMEN IN Science

# INDIAN WOMEN IN Science

Edited by
**Kaveri Shrihari**

UNBOUND SCRIPT

UNBOUND SCRIPT

# Indian Women in Science

**ISBN :** 978-93-92088-89-6



**Publisher : Unbound Script**
B-10, Seven Wonder Business Center,
Plot No. G-20, Basement, Preet Vihar,
New Delhi-110092

**Website :** www.unboundscript.com
**Email :** books@unboundscript.com

**Indian Women in Science**
*Edited by Kaveri Shrihari*
*Illustration by Nisha Rawat*

**Price** : 249/-

Printed in India

# Preface

There are many misconceptions about women in our society. One of them is that women are less logical than men. Due to this, women were kept away from the education of science and mathematics. Due to this, his contribution in this field was also ignored. Due to this, even today science and technology are not the first choice of girls. This misconceptions starts from the family and extends to the entire education system. Despite all this, women have been crossing it. Despite all this, she has made great contribution in the field of science and technology.

The journey of women scientists in India is a testament to their unwavering dedication, remarkable intellect, and unyielding determination to contribute to the advancement of knowledge and society. And their stories deserve to be told, cherished, and celebrated for the invaluable contributions.

This book-Indian women in science- delves into the lives and accomplishments of women scientists from various disciplines, spanning astronomy, physics, chemistry, biology and more. From botanist Janaki Ammal to India's first woman physician Anandibai Joshi, from the chemist Asima Chatterjee to meteorologist Anna Mani... this book covers the extraordinary spectrum of individual experiences of these women, and the complicated relationship between science and gender.

Every woman scientist in this book represents a life that dared to challenge conventions, a mind that refused to be constrained, and a spirit that soared to heights previously thought unreachable. May their stories ignite the flames of curiosity and inspire us all to explore, discover, and to create something.

# Contents

The First
Woman Physician of India

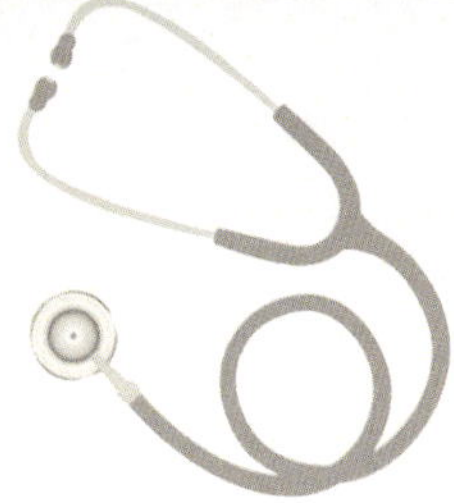

# Dr. Kadambini Ganguly

(1861-1923)

Dr. Kadambini Ganguly was the first woman physician of India. She was born on 18th July 1861 at Bhagalpur, Bihar. She was the daughter of Braja Kishore Basu, a Bramho Samaj reformer and Head Master of Bhagalpur School. The family origin was from Chandsi, in Barisal, now in Bangladesh. It is worth knowing that a special medical method was developed from this Chandni village. Which gradually spread across the country. Her father and Abhay Charan Mallick started the movement for women emancipation at Bhagalpur.

## The First Female Graduates

Kadambini started her education at the Banga Mahila Vidyalaya, and then studied at the Bethune School. Here we should know some things about this Bethune school. Bethune school was Second women's school in whole Asia. Second, because the first school was established a year earlier in 1848 by Jyotiba Phule in Pune. Later it became

Bethune College. That time it was first and only women's college in India. If you know these things, then you will understand the struggles of Kadambini.

In 1871, Kadambini became the first woman to pass the University of Calcutta Entrance Examination. The Bethune College started FA (First Arts) course for women and then graduation courses in 1883. She and Chandramukhi Basu became the first female graduates from Bethune College in the entire British Empire.

## Her Marriage and Brahmo Samaj

After her graduation, she married Brahmo Samaj reformer, a widower and leader of women's empowerment, Dwarkanath Ganguly in 1883. He was also her teacher at the Banga Mahila Vidyalaya and was twenty years older to her at the time of their marriage. The decision of their marriage was not acceptable to the Brahmo community and finally, they got married at an unknown place in Kolkata. Her husband, supporter of Women Liberation Movement encouraged her to join medical college and complete her study of medicine.

Kadambini studied medicine at the Calcutta Medical College, which started admission of women in 1883. She completed Graduate of Bengal Medical College in 1886 and became one of the two Indian women doctors to qualify for medical practice along with Anandi Gopal Joshi. She was not granted MB (Bachelor of Medicine) degree because she failed in one part of her final practical examinations. Professor R C Chandra failed her in medicine. It was believed to be a vindictive action because he opposed the inclusion of women students in Calcutta Medical College.

Then she went to United Kingdom in 1892 and qualified as LRCP (Licentiate of the Royal College of Physicians), LRCS (Licentiate of the Royal College of Surgeons) and GFPS After her return to India, she worked for a short period at the Lady Dufferin Hospital, Calcutta with a salary of Rs.300 per month. Then she started her own practice in obstetrics and gynaecology.

## A Liberated Women

She was the most accomplished and liberated Brahmo woman of her time. She kept balance between her duties towards her family as a mother and wife along with the busy schedule of the duty of a lady doctor. She had five children of her own and three children from the earlier marriage of her husband. She had two children during her studies at the Medical College, but she took minimum leave so that her medical studies were not adversely affected.

She was the first woman practicing physician of South East Asia in European medicine. She was one of the six female delegates to the Fifth Session of the Indian National Congress in 1889.

She took initiative to organise the First Women's Conference in Calcutta in 1906. She was equally interested in national politics and served as one of the first women delegates to the Indian National Congress. Today her achievements may seem small but when you think of those times, you will salute her courage. She died on 3rd October 1923 in Kolkata at the age of 62.

The first Indian woman who
received a medical degree in
western medicine

# Dr. Anandibai Joshi

(1865-1887)

The first Indian woman to receive a medical degree in western medicine was Dr. Anandibai Gopalrao Joshi. She was the first woman from India to study in the United States for two years and earn a degree in western medicine.

## Life Story

Anandibai joshi was born to a family of landlords. Her family hailed from Maharashtra and were Chitpavan Brahmins. At the tender age of nine, she was married off to a widower Gopalrao Joshi. He was a postal clerk and twenty years senior than her. He was a progressive thinker who advocated for women's education.

## Mother at 14 and The Birth Of India's First Female Doctor

When Anandi Gopal Joshi became a mother for the first time at the age of 14. Her child passed away in ten days due to a lack of resources for medical care. She made the decision to improve healthcare in India at the age of fourteen after experiencing such severe anguish and despair. She confided in her husband that her goal was to train as a doctor, a physician. He fully endorsed her desire to pursue a career in medicine.

## Support of her Husband

Anandi Joshi's husband asked an American missionary in a letter whether she might continue her education there. He even looked into finding a suitable profession for himself so he could be with her. But, Gopalrao Joshi determined and persuaded Anandi to travel to the United States alone in 1883. He urged her to serve as an inspiration for Indian women everywhere by pursuing higher education.

## Her Relentless Dedication

The Women's Medical College of Pennsylvania accepted Anandi Gopal Joshi after she submitted an application. She took a ship from Kolkata to New York. She was nineteen years old when she started her medical education. Her health, which had already suffered from her time in India, continued to deteriorate when she was in America as a result of the chilly climate and the strange food. She even had tuberculosis later on. Despite all of that, she remained driven to finish her medical degree.

Her journey had been so motivational that she received a lot of press in India. She had made history by being the first woman of Indian descent to study medicine in the country and earn a degree in it. Several generations of women have been motivated to pursue higher education by Anandi Gopal Joshi.

## Gone Too Soon

She was welcomed warmly upon her return to India in 1886 and given the position of attending physician at the Albert Edward Hospital in Kolhapur.

Anandi Gopal Joshi passed away from tuberculosis on February 26, 1887, just over a month before turning 22. India was made aware of her loss, and the entire country expressed its sorrow. The impact of Anandi gopal Joshi's struggles was so deep that many books were written on her and many films were also made. Women get strength from her struggle and her achievements.

# The First Indian Woman Botanist

# Dr. Janaki Ammal

(1897-1984)

Janaki Ammal was born in 1897 in Kerala. Her father was a judge in a subordinate court. He kept a garden in their home and wrote two books on birds in the North Malabar region of India. It was in this environment that Ammal found her affinity for the natural sciences.

As she grew up, Ammal watched as many of her sisters wed through arranged marriages. When her turn came, she made a different choice. Ammal embarked on a life of scholarship over matrimony. She went to obtaining a bachelor's degree from Queen Mary's College, Madras and an honors degree in botany from the Presidency College. It was rare for women to choose this route since women and girls were discouraged from higher education. In 1913, literacy among women in India was less than one percent, and fewer than 1,000 women in total were enrolled in school above tenth grade.

After graduating, Ammal taught for three years at the Women's Christian College in Madras. Then received a unique opportunity: to study abroad through the Barbour Scholarship, for Asian women to study in the U.S. She joined the botany department as Barbour Scholar at Michigan in 1924.

During her time at the University of Michigan she focused on genetic composition and patterns of gene expression in plants. She specialized in breeding interspecific hybrids and intergeneric hybrids. In 1925, Ammal earned a Masters of Science. In 1931, she received her doctorate, becoming the first Indian woman to receive that degree in botany in the U.S.

## Caste and Gender Discrimination

The famous scientist and Noble laureate C V Raman founded the Indian Academy of Sciences and selected Janaki as a research fellow in 1935. However, her status as a single woman from a caste considered backward created irreconcilable problems for Janaki among her male peers at Coimbatore. Facing caste and gender based discrimination, Janaki left for London where she joined the John Innes Horticultural Institute as an assistant cytologist.

## Sweetest Sugarcane in The World

Her expertise was of particular interest at the Imperial Sugar Cane Breeding Institute. The Institute was trying to bolster India's native sugarcane crop, the sweetest species of which (Saccharum officinarum) they had been importing from the island of Java. With Ammal's help, the Institute was able to develop and sustain their own sweet sugarcane varieties rather than rely on imports from Indonesia, bolstering India's sugarcane independence.

Prof. Janaki Ammal earned international recognition as a botanist of high order by her outstanding contributions in India and abroad through her extensive research and writings. She made significant investigations on cytogenetical studies of sugarcane and egg-plant and traced the evolution of these crops. Ammal worked on some of the most important genera: Solanum, Datura, Mentha, Cymbopogon and Dioscorea, besides a range of medicinal and other plants. She traced the evolution of these crops. 'Jammu Mint' is one of her major contributions.

## She made Several Intergeneric Hybrids

Ammal leaves her mark in the pages of history as a talented plant scientist who developed several hybrid crop species still grown today, including varieties of sweet sugarcane that India could grow on its own lands instead of importing from abroad. Her memory is preserved in the delicate white magnolias named after her, and a newly developed, yellow-petaled rose hybrid that now blooms in her name. In her later years, she became a forceful advocate for the value and preservation of India's native plants, earning recognition as a pioneer of indigenous approaches to the environment.

Her pioneering work on the cytogenetics of sugarcane and interspecific and intergeneric hybrids involving sugarcane and related grass species and Bambusa (bamboo) is outstanding.

She developed a garden of medicinal plants around her residence with great passion. Janaki Ammal National Award of Taxonomy was instituted by the Ministry of Environment and Forestry, The Janaki Ammal Herbarium in the Indian Institute of Integrative Medicine, Jammu has also been created in her honour.

She was an Elected Fellow, Indian National Science Academy, 1957; Fellow, Linnean Society, UK; Fellow, Royal Geographical Society, London; Fellow, Genetic Society of England; Fellow, Genetic Society of America; Fellow, Royal Horticultural Society, London; President and Secretary, Botanical Society of India, Elected Fellow and Vice-President, Indian Academy of Science, Bangalore.

She died on 7th February 1984 near Chennai. She will continue to remain an unlimited source of courage and inspiration to the younger generation of scientists.

The First
Indian Woman Anthropologist

# Irawati Karve

**(1905-1970)**

Irawati Karve was an Indian anthropologist from Maharashtra. She was born to G.H. Karmarkar, an engineer in Burma, on December 15, 1905. She was named Irawati after the great and sacred Burmese river, Irrawaddy. She grew up in Pune.

## Education and Career:

Irawati did her schooling from Pune and completed her matriculation in 1922. She received a Bachelor of Arts (Honours) degree in Philosophy in 1926 from Fergusson College, majoring in Sociology. In the same year, she married Dr. Dinkar Dhondo Karve, the son of Maharshi Karve. Under the guidance of a senior social scientist, Dr. G.S. Ghurye, she researched and submitted two essays, 'Folklore of Parshuram' and 'Chitpavan Brahman'.

Before proceeding to Germany for advanced studies, she received her Master's in Arts in Sociology from Mumbai University in 1928. She did doctoral work in anthropology from the University of Berlin, under the guidance of Eugene Fischer on the Normal Asymmetry of the Human Skull and Bones. For her researches in anthropology, Berlin University conferred on her the D. Phil, degree in 1930.

Karve served as the head of the Department of Sociology and Anthropology at Deccan College Post-Graduate and Research Institute, Pune for forty years till her retirement. She presided over the Anthropology Division of the National Science Congress held in New Delhi in 1947. She was also head of the Sociology Department at Pune University for a while.

She was invited by the Humanities Division of the Rockefeller Foundation of the United States. Chadbourne Gilpatric enabled her to undertake the trip to the US and she travelled from New York to San Francisco meeting colleagues and talking anthropology with them.

Irawati was an independent thinker and she followed her beliefs strongly. By nature, she was a researcher who preferred to work independently. She developed her personality through different media like being an assiduous professor, a researcher, an author and an orator. She was an intelligent woman who spread her knowledge.

Her enthusiasm for study, research and travel was of unmatched kind. She has the reputation of being the first woman two-wheeler driver of Pune in 1952. Her ideas of women's liberation were very modernistic. Addressing the women fighting for women's liberation, she said, "Ladies, while fighting with men for rights, why fight for only equal rights? Always fight for more rights".

After the Second World War, the fields of Cultural Anthropology and Social Anthropology were developed as independent sciences. By studying and doing in-depth research of these subjects, she successfully analysed culture and history; she was an unparalleled researcher in the world.

## Methodological Perspective:

Irawati Karve was India's first woman anthropologist at a time when anthropology and sociology were still developing as university disciplines. She was also the founder of Anthropology Department at Pune University, an indologist who mined Sanskrit texts for sociological features.

The indological tradition that Karve subscribed to was of very different from Dumont's in that there was no attempt at building or eliciting an underlying model of social relations. She belies in the importance of family, kinship, caste and religion as the basis of Indian society, and also a broad equation of Indian society with Hindu society.

# A Prominent Biochemist

# Prof. Kamala Sohonie

**(1911-1998)**

Prof. Kamala Sohonie is a scientist of international repute. She is the first Indian woman to obtain PhD from Cambridge University in 1939. She was born on 18th June 1911 in Gujarat. Her father, Narayan Rao Bhagwat, was a renowned chemist. Her sister Durga Narayan Bhagwat was an eminent Indian scholar, writer and social worker.

## Denial and Acceptence

Dr. Kamala Sohonie passed with the highest marks in the Bombay Univerity for her BSc examination. She approached Indian Institute of Science, Bangalore, but Sir C V Raman, being gender biased refused to give admission to her. Finally, she was appointed as a Probationer Staff in biochemistry with an understanding that her presence would not disturb male researchers.

After one year she was allowed to be appointed as a regular research staff. She worked under her teacher Shri Sreenivasayya, who encouraged her to carry out research on protein of milk, pulses and legumes, which had a great role to play for malnourished Indians.

## Work on Pulse Protein

She was the first researcher to work on pulse protein in 1936. She submitted her research work to the Bombay University and received the MSc degree in 1936. She was first Indian woman to get International Fellowship of the American Federation of University Women for research studies. She joined Cambridge University in 1936. She conducted valuable research during her tenure in the Cambridge

She worked in the Laboratory of Dr. Derik Richter. After some time, Dr. Richter left the Laboratory and Ms Kamala continued her research under Robin Hill on plant tissue. Her research revealed that every cell of plant tissue contained the enzyme 'Cytochrome C', which was involved in the oxidation of all plant cells. This was the original discovery, which received international acclaim among the plant research scientists.

She received two scholarships including one was at Sir William Dawn Institute of Biochemistry at the Cambridge University with the Noble Laureate Professor Fredrick Hopkins. The second one was American Travel Fellowship, which enabled her to meet eminent scientists of Europe. She submitted her thesis on 'Cytochrome C and its Role in the Respiration of Plant Tissue' to the Cambridge University.

She was the First Indian Woman to be awarded PhD in science discipline in 1939. The same year she returned to India and joined the newly opened Biochemistry Department of the Lady Hardinge College, New Delhi. Later, she became Assistant Director of the Nutrition Research Laboratory, Coonor.

She got married to Shri M V Sohonie, a professional actuary and moved to Mumbai. She joined as Faculty Member of the newly opened Department of Biochemistry at the Institute of Science, Bombay. Subsequently, she became Professor and Head of the Biochemistry Department. She became the First Director of the Institute of Science after lots of struggle and tough competition from her male counter parts.

She conducted significant research on biochemical studies on three major groups of food items consumed by rural poor and established their nutritive value. She worked hard with her students and served as a teacher and mentor of many successful researchers and distinguished scientists. She provided valuable findings on leguminous proteins, trypsin inhibitors, palm gur, palm molasses, dhanata paddy flour, etc.

## Contributions to Neera and Health Improvement

Kamala Sohonie's notable contributions revolved around her work on 'Neera,' a drink made from palm extract. This research was initiated at the suggestion of Dr. Rajendra Prasad, the first President of India. Sohonie's studies demonstrated that Neera was a rich source of Vitamin C and other vitamins, as well as sulfhydryl compounds that protected vitamins during storage. Recognizing the potential of neera as an affordable and nutritious supplement for impoverished tribal communities, she worked tirelessly to popularize its consumption. Introducing neera into the diets of malnourished tribal children and pregnant women resulted in significant health improvements.

She received award and medal for her outstanding contributions to the biochemistry and nutritional value of Neera and Palm Gur by the President of India in 1960. Dr. Kamala Sohonie passed away in 1998 at the age of 86.

## Who Studied Cosmic Rays

# Bibha Chowdhuri

**(1913-1991)**

At a time when India was fighting to break free from the shackles of colonial rule, a brilliant young woman in that very country was quietly fighting her own battles. Bibha Chowdhuri was born in 1913 in Kolkata, in erstwhile British India, into a family of social reformers. The prevailing culture of religious dogmatism and social discrimination at the time prevented women from receiving any education. Amidst such cultural stigma, Bibha's education was made possible by her progressive upbringing, which enabled her to obtain a Master's degree in physics from the University of Calcutta in 1936. She was as the only female student in her class. Later, she would become the first Indian woman to pursue a Ph.D. in physics. Her research into cosmic rays brought her very close to a Nobel Prize.

## Dwarf Star Named Bibha

A yellow-white dwarf star in the constellation Sextans, located 340 light years away, was named Bibha. Bibha means "a light beam" and refers to Bibha Chowdhuri, a pioneering Indian scientist. Bibha was the first woman researcher-faculty at the Tata Institute of Fundamental Research in 1949.

Bibha's exoplanet was christened Santamasa, a Sanskrit word that means "clouded", which refers to the nature of the exoplanet's atmosphere. US space agency Nasa defines exoplanets as planets that orbit around stars outside our solar system.

The names of the two astronomical bodies were announced by the Paris-based International Astronomical Union along with the names of 111 sets of exoplanets and host stars.

## A Ray of Light

She moved to the Bose institute when Dr. Bose shifted there from University of Calcutta and published three major papers during her time there. Her research during this period was focused on cosmic rays as they were the only source of subatomic particles back then.

Without any particle accelerators, people back then used to go to top of mountains and try to study subatomic particles in these rays using cloud chambers. A cloud chamber is an enclosed instrument which keeps ethanol or other substance in vapor state. If a high energy particle travels through this chamber, it leaves a trail like aeroplanes do in the sky. You can study these trails to find out their charge, mass, and momentum. Such trails are very short lived however and there weren't many ways to study them before they vanished.

Dr Bose and Bibha solved this problem by using photographic plates which could capture the trails of subatomic particles traveling through them. They placed such plates on two mountains of different elevation. This allowed them to study not only the subatomic particles but also how they decayed while traveling through the atmosphere.

About seven years later, a British physicist, Dr. Cecil Frank Powell did the same experiment with better plates. He received the Nobel Prize for his discovery of Pi Masons and Muons. In his book, Dr. Powell acknowledged Bibha and C M Bose's research and their experiment. His results on the mass of these particles were also very similar to the ones calculated by Bibha during her research. She returned to her birth city, Kolkata, where she was to spend the rest of her days. She remained active in science till her death in 1991.

An Indian Organic Chemist

# Dr. Asima Chatterjee

(1917-2006)

Dr. Asima Chatterjee was one of the leading scientists of the country. She made pioneering contributions in the field of organic chemistry. She was born on 23rd September 1917 in Kolkata to the family of Dr. Indra Narayan Mukherjee. She received early inspiration from her family to pursue higher education. She joined Scottish Church College, Calcutta and graduated in Chemistry with Honours in 1936. She pursued MSc from Calcutta University in 1938.

She joined DSc at Calcutta University and completed her research in 1944. She visited USA to conduct Postdoctoral Research at the University of Wisconsin. She was awarded DSc for her significant research contributions in the field of her specialization from University of Burdwan and Banaras Hindu University.

Dr. Asima Chatterjee worked in various capacities and held prestigious teaching positions. She was Professor and Head of the Chemistry Department, Lady Brabourne College, Calcutta, 1940-54; Reader, Department of Pure Chemistry, University College of Science, Calcutta University, 1954-61; Head of Chemistry Department, Calcutta University, 1969-79; Khaira Professor of Chemistry, University of

Calcutta, 1962-82; Professor of Pure Chemistry, University College of Science and Technology, Calcutta, 1962-82; and Nominated Member of Rajya Sabha, 1982-90.

Dr. Chatterjee conducted immense research work in the field of natural products, specially alkaloids, polyphenolics, terpenoids and coumarins derived from Indian medicinal plants.

She imbibed the interest in Indian medicinal plants from her father Indra Narayan Mukherjee, a doctor having interest in making use of traditional medicinal herbs. During her research studies abroad, she gained extensive research experience on naturally occurring glycosides, carotinoids and provitamines and biologically active alkaloids, which became her life long passion for research.

## What is Ayush-56

She made notable contributions in the field of medicinal chemistry, analytical chemistry and mechanistic organic chemistry. Her research findings on hydramine fission reaction has been included in standard textbooks in chemistry. She isolated a number of physiologically active compounds from Indian plants such as the anti-epileptic drug, Ayush-56 from Marsilia minuta and the anti-malarial drug from Alstonia scholaris, Swertia chirata, Picrorphiza kurroa and Ceasalpinna crista. The patented drugs have been marketed by several companies.

Through her untiring efforts, Dr. Chatterjee could establish a Regional Research Institute, Central Council for Research in Ayurveda and Siddha inKolkata for carrying out research on Indian medicinal plants for the development of Ayurvedic drugs along with an Ayurvedic Hospital for systematic clinical trials under the control of the Ministry of Health and Family Welfare. As the Honorary Principal coordinator, she nurtured the Institute till the end of her life.

## As a Rajya Sabha Member

Dr. Chatterjee was the first woman to be conferred with the Doctorate Degree by an Indian University, Calcutta University in 1944. She was the first woman General President of the Indian Science Congress Association in 1975. She was also the first woman scientist to be nominated as the Rajya Sabha Member in 1982. She served in various capacities for national level commissions and committees. And ahe is recipient of various prestigious laurels.

## As a Torchbearer

Throughout her career, Kamala Sohonie faced gender bias and discrimination. However, she remained steadfast in her pursuit of scientific excellence and paved the way for future generations of women in science. Her achievements and advocacy played a vital role in challenging prevailing stereotypes and inspiring young women to pursue scientific careers. Sohonie passed away on June 28, 1998, leaving behind a legacy of resilience, determination, and groundbreaking research.

An Indian Meteorologist

# Anna Mani

**(1918-2001)**

As India and the world debate a severe underrepresentation of girls and women in science, the story of Anna Mani, a pioneering woman scientist from India, should not be left out of the discussion. She Born in 1918 in a Syrian Christian family, Anna Mani grew up in Kerala and made several contributions in the field of physics and metrology. Her contribution made it possible for India to make a path for accurate weather forecasts and lay the groundwork to harness renewable energy. Her contributions changed the way India gauges weather; she even helped lay the ground for harnessing solar and wind power as alternative sources of energy.

Her father was a civil engineer. The Mani's family was a typical upper-class professional household, where from childhood the male children were groomed for high-level careers, whereas the daughters were primed for marriage. But Anna Mani would have none of it. Instead, she spent years immersed in books and decided to forge her own path. Instead of marrying early like her sisters she opted for higher education. She wore khadi all her life.

Anna Mani graduated with a B.Sc Honours degree in Physics and Chemistry from Chennai in 1939. Post-graduation, she worked closely under Professor CV Raman and was involved in researching the optical properties of ruby and diamond. Around that time, she also authored about five research papers but was not recognised or granted a PhD for her works as she did not have a master's degree in Physics. Proving her capacities yet once again, she moved to Britain to pursue her master's, as required, in 1945. However, here she found her interest in studying meteorological instruments and picked up the course at the Imperial College, London.

Returning to India in 1948, she joined the Meteorological department in Pune. From this post, she published numerous research papers on meteorological instrumentation. These works are known to have set the base in the coming years for the country to make accurate forecasts and harness their renewable energy sources to their optimum capacity. Anna Mani standardised the drawings for nearly 100 different weather instruments and started their production. she set up a network of stations in India to measure solar radiation. She also published a number of papers on subjects ranging from atmospheric ozone to the need for international instrument comparisons and national standardisation Her interest in the subject was fuelled by her wish to make India independent in weather instrumentation.

She was made the head of the division at the Meteorological Department, which was a space considered to be male-dominated with a team of over 100 men. Under her guidance, the department was able to produce so many simplified and standardised weather instruments and other indigenous infrastructure for forecasting. She established a small workshop in Bangalore to manufacture instruments for measuring wind speed and solar energy. The workshop was also the space where she developed an apparatus to measure ozone.

She also published several papers on sustainable energy measurement, which made her one of the earliest advocates for sustainable energy in the country.

She relentlessly worked towards the development of science and tech in the country and held pivotal positions in organisations, including the United Nations World Meteorological Organization, Indian National Science Academy, American Meteorological Society, International Ozone Association, International Solar Energy Society, and so on. In 1987, she became a recipient of the INSA K. R. Ramanathan Medal for her impeccable contributions to science. She passed away on August 16, 2001, but her legacies continue to live through the many works.

First
Woman Engineer from Karnataka

# Prof. Rajeswari Chatterjee

**(1922-2010)**

Prof. Rajeshwari Chatterjee is one of the pioneering women who helped pave the way for women scientists and engineers in India. She is the first woman engineer from Karnataka, with significant contributions to the field of microwave and antennae engineering.

## Her Grandmother

Rajeshwari Chatterjee was born during the British Raj to an upper class family which included her social activist grandmother, Smt Kamalamma Dasappa. Though widowed at the young age of 20, Kamalamma pursued higher education graduating with a BA and spent the rest of her life promoting women's education at a time when it was discouraged due to marriage requirements. Smt Kamalamma Dasappa started an experimental school in Mahila Seva Samaj for widows, deserted wives and young girls. This school provided an accelerated program to finish secondary education by the age of 14. Rajeshwari's early education was from this school, and encouraged by her grandmother, she pursued postsecondary education completing her BSc (c. 1939) and MSc (c1942) in Mathematics.

## Denial

Rajeshwari applied to the Indian Institute for Science (IISc) to work under CV Raman but was denied due to lack of degrees in Physics. This was not to deter the determined Rajeshwari, and after extensive debate about the female candidate, she was able to join as a research student in Communication Engineering under SP Chakravarty at the Department of Electrical Technology.

In the early 1940s, India had an interim government in Delhi as the British prepared to leave the country. During this time, a scientific committee consisting of many of India's best-known scientists prompted this government to start a scholarship program for talented Indian students in science and engineering to research abroad in USA, Britain and Canada.

Rajeshwari won this prestigious scholarship in 1946. A month before independence, Rajeshwari boarded a ship to the US as an unmarried woman in her 20s with the full support of her family. The scholarship required her to serve the newly formed India for at least 3 years upon the completion of her studies.

Rajeshwari earned a Masters from the Department of Electrical Engineering. followed by 8-month practical training in Division of Radio Frequency Measurements at the National Bureau of Standards in Washington DC. In c.1953, Rajeshwari completed her PhD under Prof. William G. Dow. She was the first woman engineer of the Karnataka state.

## Return to India

On her return to India in 1953, she started her teaching career as Assistant Professor, at the Department of Electrical Communication Engineering, Indian Institute of Science, Bangalore. Later, she was promoted to the level of Professor and Chairman, and served the same institute until her retirement.

She married Dr. Sisir Kumar Chatterjee, whom she knew for some years. As both of them were in the same department, they dedicated their service to build up the well-equipped Microwave Laboratory for the first time in India. Professor Chatterjee played a pioneering role to initiate teaching and research in the field of microwave engineering. She was the first woman professor of engineering at the Indian Institute of Science, Bangalore. She conducted teaching and research in electromagnetic theory, electron tube circuits, etc. She received many awards for her research work.

She published over 100 research papers and seven books on microwave engineering and antennae. She authored the book 'A Thousand Streams: A Personal History' narrating sociological plight of Indian women facing gender and cast discrimination.

She made outstanding research contributions in the field of antennae, mainly for aircraft and space craft applications. She died on 3rd September 2010.

An Indian Oceanograp

# Aditi Pant

(1943)

For so long, the male scientists dominated the tech world in all aspects. Women are overlooked when men are at the helm of things. But, that doesn't mean that there is space for male chauvinism. Women have a lot of catching up to do. They are making every possible attempt to carve out a reputation for themselves as successful people.

Women scientists are very rare in number and there aren't many who are extending their services in the field of science. As far as their presence is concerned, they have made significant contributions to scientific discovery and pushed the boundaries beyond human knowledge. They have gone through struggles seeking education, finding jobs. But they have overcome these difficulties to come through with flying colours.

One among such women who made a position for themselves in the world of history is Dr. Aditi Pant. She was the first Indian woman to visit the farthest corner of the world, the Antarctica region. She was an oceanographer who made the nation proud by being the first woman to set the foot on the icy terrains of the Antarctica.

## The Open Sea

She born in Nagpur, not much is known about her early life but the information about her educational career is enough to show how brilliant and wonderful lady Dr. Aditi Pant was. She finished her B.Sc. from the University of Pune. While her undergraduate studies, Aditi Pant came across the book named 'The Open Sea' by Alister Hardy. This book had a very big effect in her life and that was when she decided to take up oceanography as her career.

The firm determination of Aditi Pant of being an oceanographer was boosted up with the US government scholarship to study Masters in marine sciences in the University of Hawaii. She pursued her PhD in Physiology in Marine Algae from the Westfield College in University of London.

Women were not allowed to get a very good education that time. But Dr. Anita Pant had set up an example to the women section that not only can women reach up to space but also face the severe challenges of the ocean. After finishing her education, Dr. Anita Pant started working with the National Institute of Oceanography situated in Goa. From 1973 to 1976, Aditi Pant studied a lot about the coasts and toured the Western Coastal areas of India. She also worked with the National Chemical Laboratory in Pune.

## Third Expedition

Dr. Aditi Pant was the first Indian lady to join the Third Expedition of the Antarctica region in the year 1983. She worked as a part of the Indian Antarctic Programme to explore the cold and chilled regions of the Antarctica. Under the severe and rough weather conditions Dr. Aditi Pant analysed the continent for four months and came out with wonderful discoveries.

The marvellous woman Dr. Aditi Pant was honoured by the Antarctica Award for being a part of the expedition. She was a wonderful and a very strong woman who is an inspiration for all other women around the nation to do what they want to and to achieve success everywhere, no matter which part of the Universe it is!

## Pioneer of In-vitro Fertilization

# Dr. Indira Hinduja

(1946)

Urbanization rates have also increased infertility rates globally, and in India, up to 14% of the Indian population is impacted by infertility. Artificial reproductive technologies have made great advancements in the last 40 years. Dr. Indira Hinduja has been on the forefront of it in India.

Dr. Indira Hinduja was born on 18th December 1943 at Shikarpur, Pakistan. Her parents migrated from Pakistan, when she was just a few months old. Initially, her family settled in Belgaun, and then shifted to Bombay in 1963. Dr. Hinduja took her school education at Mahila Vidyalaya, Belgaun and obtained MBBS from Topiwala National Medical College and B Y L Nair Hospital, Bombay in 1967. Later she obtained DGO (Diploma in Obstetrics and Gynaecology), College of Physicians and Surgeons, Bombay in 1969; DFP (Diploma in Family Planning), College of Physicians and Surgeons, Bombay in 1970; MD (Obstetrics and Gynaecology), University of Bombay, Bombay in

1972. She also did PhD in Applied Biology from University of Bombay, Bombay in 1988 where she presented her thesis on Human In Vitro Fertilization (IVF) and Embryo Transfer.

She started her career as Clinical Faculty Member of the Seth G S Medical College and KEM Hospital. She joined BYL Nair Charitable Hospital, Topiwala National Medical (TNM) College, Bombay as House Physician in Department of Pediatrics in 1967. Then served as House Surgeon at the Department of Obstetrics and Gynaecology of the hospital from 1967-68. She became the Registrar of the Preventive and Social Medicine at the hospital (1968-69) and then Registrar of the Department of Obstetrics and Gynaecology from 1969-72. Later, she became the Senior Registrar of the Department of Obstetrics and Gynaecology, King Edward Memorial

She was Professor, Department of Obstetrics and Gynaecology, KEM Hospital, Seth GS Medical College Bombay from 1987-91; Honorary Obstetrician and Gynaecologist (IVF and Infertility specialist), Department of Obstetrics and Gynaecology, Jaslok Hospital and Research Centre, Bombay, 1991-till date; Honorary Obstetrician and Gynaecologist (IVF specialist) at Department of Obstetric & Gynaecology, PD Hinduja National Hospital & Research Centre, Mumbai; Scientific Director and Co-founder of INKUS IVF Centre, Bombay.

Dr. Hinduja won many laurels from India and abroad for her outstanding research contributions. In 1986, the Greater Bombay conferred on her the Mayor's Award. She was also awarded Young Indian Award, 1987; Outstanding Lady Citizen of Maharashtra State Jaycee Award, 1987; Rotary International Public Vocational Excellence Trophy, 1994; Bharat Nirman Award, 1994; International Women's Day Award by the Mayor of Mumbai, 1995 and 2000; Lifetime Achievement Award, Federation of Obstetrics and Gynaecological Society of India,

1999; Dhanwantri Award, Government of Maharashtra, 2000; Indira Appreciation Momento, 2001; and Padma Shri, 2011.

## Reproductive Health Research

While working on IVF, Indira also pioneered the gamete intrafallopian transfer (GIFT) technology where the egg is fertilized in the fallopian tubes. The first GIFT baby was born on January 4th, 1988. In addition, Indira is also credited for developing an oocyte donation technique for menopausal and premature ovarian failure patients, giving the country's first baby out of this technique on January 24th, 1991.

In 1989, Indira with her colleague, Dr. Kusum Zaveri, started the Inkus IVF Centre in southern Mumbai. Initially, they conducted their research and treatment at their facility and later established a practice at P D Hinduja Hospital in Mumbai in 2011.

Indira's research revolves around reproductive health and understanding male and female infertility. Understanding cytogenetics (chromosomal abnormalities) in infertile men and the correlation with artificial reproductive technologies has advanced our understanding of reproduction in humans. Furthermore, her work has also paved the way into stem cell biology with pioneering work in embryonic stem cells, somatic nuclear transfer and pluripotent stem cells in adult ovaries called Very Small Embryonic-like Stem cells (VSELs). These VSELs may produce gametes which would further benefit many people with the dream of parenthood. Till date, Indira has helped over 15,000 couples with IVF treatment alone!

## First Indian Woman in Space

# Kalpana Chawla

(1962-2003)

Human fascination with space is as old as humans. Imagine a human eye capturing the vastness of space, and the mind trying to make sense of it. It is overwhelming, putting it too softly. Poetry, philosophy, mysticism and religious episteme – all have engaged with space, with heavens, and with heavenly bodies. There was a time when heavenly bodies were deified. It still is at places, but the progress in science leaves little space for such beliefs now. Science has shown the way to conquer the space, to land on moon, to send mission to mars. All those great scientists who probed into space and added to our knowledge of universe are our leaders. Calpna Chawala is One of them. who said: "When you look at the stars and the galaxy, you feel that you are not just from any particular piece of land, but from the solar system."

Kalpana Chawla was born on 17th March 1962 at Karnal, Haryana. She was the daughter of Bansi Lal Chawla and Sanyogita and the youngest of the four children in the family.

She completed her school education from the Karnal. She was fascinated by aircraft and flying as a child. She used to accompany her father to local flying clubs to see the planes. She obtained (BTech, Aeronautics) from the Punjab Engineering College, Chandigarh in 1982. To realize her ambitious dream, she moved to USA and joined Postgraduate Studies in the University of Texas, USA in 1984; Doctoral Studies in Aerospace Engineering, University of Colorado, USA, 1988. She took Commercial Pilot's Training and became Flight Instructor with airplane and glider ratings. She obtained Commercial Pilot's License for single and multiple engine, land and sea planes, and gliders.

## Fascination for Sky

She was determined to achieve something different and new. She had a great fascination for sky, stars and planets. Quite often she opted for making models related to outer space and heavenly bodies in her school projects. She was the first woman to be enrolled for Aeronautical Engineering in the Punjab Engineering College, Chandigarh. In September 1982, she travelled to USA for higher education. She married Jean-Pierre Harrison, a Frenchman and flying instructor in 1983. She became naturalized citizen of America in April 1991.

She worked as Research Scientist at MCAT Institute (San Jose, California) to support research in the area of powered lift at NASA Ames Research Centre, California in 1988. She was responsible for simulation and analysis of flow physics pertaining to the operations of powered-lift air craft such as the Harrier in ground effect. At Overset Methods Inc., California, she worked on simulation of moving multiple body problems. She was responsible for the development and implementation of efficient techniques to perform aerodynamic optimization, and smooth take off.

## An Astronaut

She was selected by NASA as an astronaut in 1994. She was one of the 19 finalist candidates from 2962 applications at the Johnson Space Centre, NASA. She had to go through rigorous training including learning to fly a supersonic jet, parachute jump, ejection seat operations, week long survival course, etc. She was trained in simulated microgravity operations at a long swimming pool described as neutral density tank. But she could not pass the extra-vehicular activity in space, because she was found too small for space suit meant for extra vehicular activity—commonly known as a Space Walk.

She was assigned the job on technical issues for astronaut office EVA/Robotics and Computer branches. She was finally included as a mission specialist on the crew of the fourth US Microgravity Payload Flight-Mission STS-87. The Columbia Mission started on 10th November 1997 and returned successfully on 5th December 1997.

## The Columbia Mission

Thirteen years later, she was again given an opportunity by the NASA as a crew member for STS-107. The space shuttle was originally scheduled to be launched on 11th May 2000, but due to various reasons it was delayed and it launched on 16th January 2003.

This was on the morning of February 1 when everyone at the Kennedy Space Center in Cape Canaveral was waiting for the Columbia to return smoothly to earth after spending 15 days in the vacuum of space. LeRoy Cain, NASA's Entry Flight Director, had given the final green light to Shuttle commander Rick Husband to start the de-orbit and reentry procedures for descent STS-107. This was the start to end the Columbia's 28th mission to space.

## What Happened?

After the initiation of the reentry procedure of Columbia, telemetry indicated that the hydraulic fluid temperatures went off-scale low, and nothing could point out or explain the fault. In contrast, all the other hydraulic system indications were good. This off-scale low fluid temperature caused a sudden loss in tire pressure on the left side, which made the shuttle almost impossible to land due to not having proper tire pressure.

As per the reports by Space Safety Magazine, with each passing second, more and more sensors in Columbia started to malfunction, leading to the loss of all kinds of communication. Efforts of reestablishing contact with the radar and relocating the spacecraft by Houston failed. The disaster was struck by then, and the reports of people spotting fireballs in the sky hit the headlines making the biggest nightmare of the team come to life.

Commander Michael P. Anderson, Mission Specialists David M. Brown, Kalpana Chawla, and Laurel B. Clark, and Payload Specialist Ilan Ramon of the Israeli Space Agency, adding Commander Rick D. Husband and Pilot William C. "Willie" McCool were among the 7 astronauts who died in this tragedy.

The Shuttle program was shut for two years following the Columbia disaster. An intense investigation was launched, revealing that the beginning of this tragedy happened on the day of its take-off itself. The spacecraft wing was breached because a large piece of foam had fallen from the shuttle's external tank.

Right after 82 seconds of launching the shuttle from Cape Canaveral, the piece of foam fell and was later seen striking the wing of the spacecraft. It was later revealed that the hole caused atmospheric gases to bleed into the shuttle as it went ahead with its reentry to the earth leading to the sensor loss and eventually the disaster.

The world saw the whole incident on television sets across the globe.

During her two space missions, Kalpana spent 30 days, 14 hours and 54 minutes in space. She was the first Indian born American woman to enter space in 1997. Kalpana's death certificate mentioned the place of death as 'Airspace over Texas'. She was dressed in a blue NASA flight suit before cremation.

Her story of the bravest woman of India became an inspiring legend for younger generation. She has been posthumously awarded the Congressional Space Medal of Honour; NASA Space Flight Medal; and the NASA Distinguished Service Medal. Though she is physically not present with us, even then her courage and dream will continue to inspire many young children back home to achieve something different and special in their life.

Are you inspired by women like Kalpana Chawla? Would you like to fly into space or be the first to accomplish a goal? Dare to dream big!

Rocket Woman of India

# Ritu Karidhal

**(1975)**

India's ambitious lunar mission, Chandrayaan-3, successfully touched down on the lunar surface on August 23, marking a monumental achievement for the nation's space programme. Amid the celebrations for the historic achievement of the Indian Space Research Organisation, from common people to politicians. All are praising the team of scientists behind the Chandrayaan-3 mission. Nearly 54 women engineers and scientists were part of the Chandrayaan-3 mission and they handled several important responsibilities. The Chandrayaan-3 mission was headed by senior scientist Dr Ritu Karidhal.

## From Physics to Lunar Landing

Popularly known as the "rocket woman" of India, Ritu Karidhal is from Lucknow. She pursued a Bachelor's degree in Physics from Lucknow University. Later, she received her ME in Aerospace Engineering from Indian Institute of Science. Dr. Srivastava cracked the Graduate Aptitude Test in Engineering (GATE) six months into her Ph.D. This marked a turning point, prompting her to leave her PhD studies behind and venture into space exploration. Guided by her professor, Manisha Gupta, she joined ISRO.

At the UR Rao Satellite Centre, her educational background and exceptional performance at IISc catapulted her into challenging roles, where she fearlessly tackled advanced projects usually reserved for senior scientists. Dr. Ritu says that she was being given projects that were very advanced even when there were senior scientists available. This early recognition and trust fuelled her confidence and ignited her passion for the field.

Dr Ritu Karidhal Srivastava's leadership journey at the ISRO started with her appointment as the Deputy Mission Director of the Mars Orbiter Mission (MOM) - Mangalyaan-1. This historical mission, launched on November 5, 2013, marked India's first interplanetary endeavour.

Subsequently, she took over as the Mission Director of Chandrayaan-2, successfully launched on July 22, 2019. Her most recent achievement, leading Chandrayaan-3, marks another milestone in her illustrious career.

Ritu Karidhal was awarded the ISRO Young Scientist Award in 2007 by the then-president of India, A.P.J. Abdul Kalam. She was presented with the ISRO Team Award in 2015 for her important role in Mangalyaan's success. Ritu Karidhal was also listed in BBC's prestigious "100 Women" list for shattering gender biases in the STEM field. She was also appointed to a newly formed Gender Equality Advisory Council (GEAC) by United Kindom's Minister for Women and Equalities Liz Truss when the country assumed the presidency of the G7 in 2021. Other awards included the ASI Team Award, Women Achievers in Aerospace, 2017 by the Society of Indian Aerospace Technologies & Industries.

# Some Other Prominent

**Dr. Sita Acharya**
A well-known Obstetrician and Gynaecologist.

**Padmavati Bandopadhay**
The first woman doctor to become aviation medicine specialist.

**Shakuntala Bhagat**
A renowned engineer.

**Dr. Padam Kumari Agarwal**
A renowned Physician and Pathologist.

**Sneh Bhargava**
Distinct contribution as an outstanding medical scientist and educationist.

**Katherlsetl Indira Bai**
A noted Pediatrician and Neurologist.

**Yamuna Krishnan**
Chemical scientist

**Sujatha Ramadorai**
An internationaly acclaimed algebraic number theorist.

**Karimpat Mathangi Ramakrishnan**
An eminent personality in the field of plastic surgery.

**Shashi Wadhwa**
A distinguished Anatomist in India.

**Kamal Jaysing Ranadive**
An eminent personality in the filed of cell and molecular biology.

**Sheela K Ramasesha**
Notable contibution in the field of chemistry and material science.